HIGH-IMPACT RESOURCES FOR PEAK PERFORMERS

Single Seat Mindset is designed specifically for peak performers that desire cutting-edge ideas from some of the world's most elite fighter pilots. I would like to extend a personal invitation for you to be a part of our independent minded community.

You can get all of that and more through our resources... most of which are no cost to you! Additionally, you can contact us directly to ask your questions that deserve a unique perspective unlike anything found anywhere else in the world...a fighter pilot's perspective.

If you are a peak performer with a *"Let's get it done, don't hold me back,"* attitude and want immediate results, please visit us at:

SingleSeatMindset.com

Put your talents to good use and accelerate past all the slow people holding you back from your ambitious goals.

Blog.SingleSeatMindset.com

If you are a fighter pilot and would like to become part of our team, please contact us here to become an elite guide and give back for all of your above average experiences:

SingleSeatMindset.com/contact

SINGLE SEAT GRATITUDE

A GIFT FROM

DOMINIC "SLICE" TEICH

Single Seat Mindset leverages the backgrounds of fighter pilots to help motivated peak performers maximize their talents with the most cutting-edge approach towards achieving worthwhile life goals—BE Somebody.

SingleSeatMindset.com

CONTENTS

Attitude Is Altitude 1

PART 1
Gratitude Quotes 5

PART 2
Pilot Quotes 27

PART 3
Inspirational Quotes..51

PART 4
Humorous Quotes 77

PART 5
The Path Forward 97
How We Help Peak Performers Become
Even More Successful...99
The Next Step 101
About Dominic "Slice" Teich 103
About Single Seat Mindset 107
A Small Request..109
Want to Give Back? 111

ACKNOWLEDGEMENT

To Joe and Polly Schindler. Your drive to help families with children riddled with cancer has influenced me in ways I never imagined. Your journey that started when your daughter Anna was diagnosed due to Hepatoblastoma in 2010 has influenced and shaped the lives of so many; even with the loss of your baby girl, Anna.

Thank you for being a positive influence in my life. We named our baby girl Anna so that her memory can carry on with the Anna Schindler Foundation. 100% of the proceeds from any of our books will go directly to your foundation to help families that are going through what you have already painfully endured. God bless your drive and determination to make the world a better place. It has inspired me to be a better version of myself. Learn more at:

AnnaSchindlerFoundation.org

ATTITUDE IS ALTITUDE

"Once you have tasted flight,
you will forever walk the earth with your eyes
turned skyward, for there you have been, and there
you will always long to return."
–Leonardo da Vinci

THANK YOU!

The very fact you have received this little book means you are very important to me. I appreciate you. This relationship means so much to me that I wanted to express my gratitude by giving you a little guide that will help you snap out of any trials or tribulations that the day may throw at you.

My daily journey begins by realizing the importance of being grateful for all the people, gifts, and blessings we have in our individual lives. I try to pause often and remind myself just how fortunate I am, regardless of the number of things that I am able to accumulate. This short book can help you remember to be thankful for the life that you have and also remind you to pause at the end of the day to remember what means most to you in your life. This positive attitude and short, helpful habit that you will generate will help you in more ways that you know and also enable you to see all the bright things in each situation even if the immediate 'good' isn't seen.

Single Seat Gratitude is a collection of wise quotes and thoughts from people throughout history. As a single seat F-16 fighter pilot, I've spent a great deal of time thinking about which quotes I actually wanted to be in this book because they express ideas, thoughts and reminders that inspire me on a daily basis and help me to reframe every situation towards a more powerful mindset.

This book isn't meant to be read cover-to-cover but rather a resource to go to when you need a quick fighter pilot style boost of inspiration; gentle reminders to keep you moving in a positive direction. Keep this in a convenient place as it will work in wonderous ways when you take a short pause throughout the day to contemplate the wisdom that already exists within your own heart.

My hope and positive intention is to make you see that I appreciate you being in my life. If you ever need another copy of *Single Seat Gratitude*, just reach out to me and I would be happy to send you another one at no cost, and if you would like to share your story, I would love to hear how you tackled life's trials and tribulations and turned them into a victory.

To your success,

Dominic "Slice" Teich

SingleSeatMindset.com

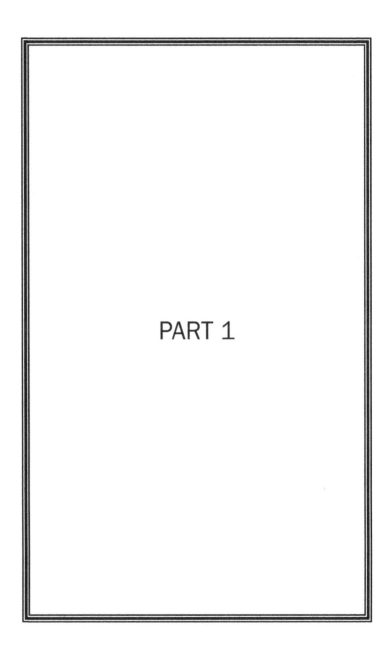

PART 1

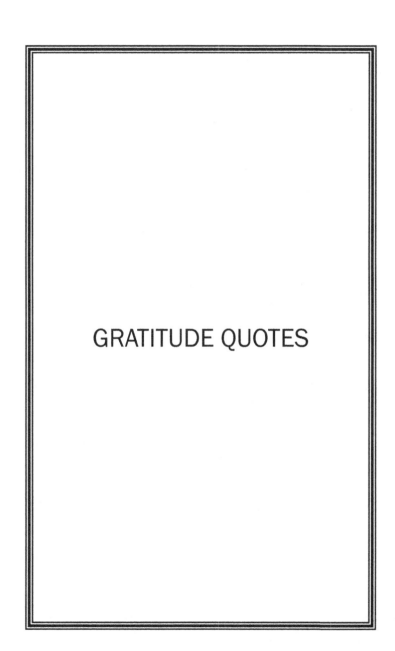

GRATITUDE QUOTES

"Gratitude transforms what we have today into enough."

–Mike Capuzzi

"Gratitude is the healthiest of all human emotions. The more you express gratitude for what you have, the more likely you will have even more to express gratitude for."

–Zig Ziglar

"Enjoy the little things, for one day you may look back and realize they were the big things."

–Robert Brault

"Feeling gratitude and not expressing it is like wrapping a present and not giving it."

–William Arthur Ward

"The way to develop the best that is in a person is by appreciation and encouragement."

–Charles Schwab

"When I started counting my blessings, my whole life turned around."

–Willie Nelson

"The roots of all goodness lie in the soil of appreciation for goodness."

–Dalai Lama

"There are only two ways to live your life. One is as though nothing is a miracle. The other is as though everything is a miracle."

–Albert Einstein

"Reflect upon your present blessings, of which every man has plenty; not on your past misfortunes, of which all men have some."

–Charles Dickens

"None is more impoverished than the one who has no gratitude. Gratitude is a currency that we can mint for ourselves, and spend without fear of bankruptcy."

–Fred De Witt Van Amburgh

"Some people grumble that roses have thorns; I am grateful that thorns have roses."

–Alphonse Karr

"It is through gratitude for the present moment that the spiritual dimension of life opens up."

–Eckhart Tolle

"Gratitude is a duty which ought to be paid,
but which none have a right to expect."

–Jean-Jacques Rousseau

"Happiness cannot be traveled to, owned, earned, worn or consumed. Happiness is the spiritual experience of living every minute with love, grace, and gratitude."

–Denis Waitley

"Gratitude bestows reverence, allowing us to encounter everyday epiphanies, those transcendent moments of awe that change forever how we experience life and the world."

–John Milton

"Sometimes we should express our gratitude
for the small and simple things like the scent
of the rain, the taste of your favorite food, or
the sound of a loved one's voice."

–Joseph Wirthlin

"Gratitude is riches. Complaint is poverty."

–Doris Day

"Of all the characteristics needed for both a happy and morally decent life, none surpasses gratitude. Grateful people are happier, and grateful people are more morally decent."

–Dennis Prager

THOUGHTS

SINGLE SEAT GRATITUDE

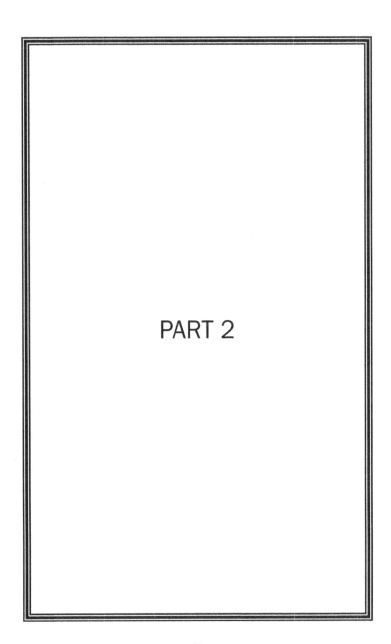

PART 2

PILOT QUOTES

"Please dear God, don't let me mess this up."

—Every Pilot in a Tight Spot

"Getting high is my job."

−Anonymous

"Being a pilot doesn't make you cool but if you're cool, you're probably a pilot."

–Anonymous

"Flying is learning how to throw yourself at the ground and miss."

–Douglas Adams

"The engine is the heart of an airplane, but the pilot is its soul."

–Walter Raleigh

"Pilots take no special joy in walking.
Pilots like flying."

—Neil Armstrong

"When everything seems to be going against you, remember that an airplane takes off against the wind, not with it."

–Henry Ford

"Aviation is proof that given the will, we have the capacity to achieve the impossible."

–Eddie Rickenbacker

"I think it is a pity to lose the romantic side of flying and simply to accept it as a common means of transportation."

–Amy Johnson

"Flying is more than a sport and more than a job; flying is pure passion and desire, which will fill a lifetime."

–Adolf Galland

"Allow your passion to become your purpose,
and it will one day become your profession."

–Gabrielle Bernstein

"When in doubt, hold your altitude; nobody
ever collided with the sky."

—Anonymous

"Fighter pilots have ice in their veins. They don't have emotions. They think, anticipate. They know that fear and other concerns cloud your mind from what's going on and what you should be involved in."

−Buzz Aldrin

"Every takeoff is optional.
Every landing is mandatory."

—Anonymous

"Airspeed, altitude, and brains. Two are always
needed to successfully complete the flight."

–Anonymous

"Both optimists and pessimists contribute to
our society. The optimist invents the airplane
and the pessimist the parachute."

–Gil Stern

"You've never been lost until you've been lost
at Mach 3."

–Paul Crickmore

"Learn from the mistakes of others. You won't live long enough to make all of them yourself."

–Anonymous

"You start with a bag full of luck and an empty bag of experience. The trick is to fill the bag of experience before you empty the bag of luck."

–Anonymous

"Good judgement comes from experience.
Unfortunately, the experience usually comes
from bad judgement."

–Anonymous

THOUGHTS

SINGLE SEAT GRATITUDE

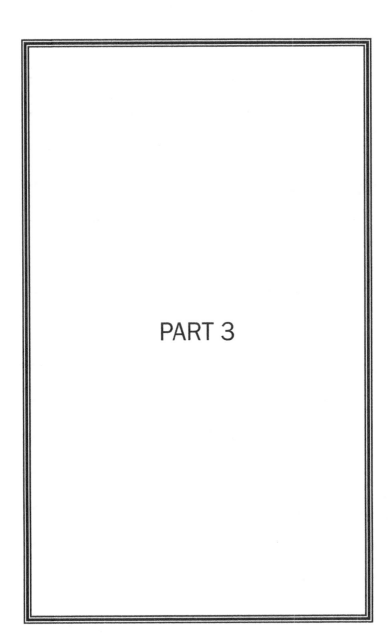

PART 3

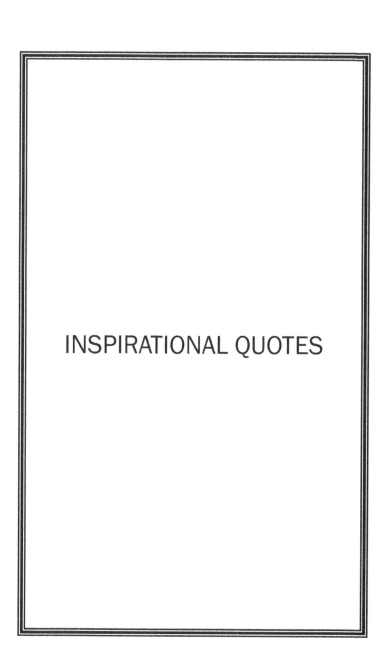

INSPIRATIONAL QUOTES

"Eliminate the time between the idea and the act, and your dreams will become reality."

–Dr. Edward L. Kramer

"My life is one long obstacle course, with me being the chief obstacle."

–Jack Paar

"There is only one success—to be able to
spend your life in your own way."

–Christopher Morley

"The only thing that some people do is grow older."

–Edgar Howe

"The secret to living is giving."

—Tony Robbins

"On an important decision one rarely has 100% of the information needed for a good decision no matter how much one spends or how long one waits. And, if one waits too long, he has a different problem and has to start all over. This is the terrible dilemma of the hesitant decision maker."

–Robert Greenleaf

"Hope is not a strategy."

–Vince Lombardi

"Strategy is a commodity; execution is an art."

–Peter Drucker

"The difference between try and triumph is a little umph."

–Zig Ziglar

"You can't eat money but you can't eat without it."

–Chinese Proverb

"Believe that problems do have answers, that they can be overcome, and that we can solve them."

–Norman Vincent Peale

"One of the great lessons in life is to know that even fools are right sometimes."

–Winston Churchill

"Without strategy, execution is aimless.
Without execution, strategy is useless."

–Morris Chang

"Your imagination is your preview of life's coming attractions."

–Albert Einstein

"To accomplish great things, we must not only act, but also dream, not only plan, but also believe."

–Anatole France

"Everything happens for you, not to you. Learn to reframe and you'll never lose."

–Hal Elrod

"Experience is not what happens to you.
Experience is what you DO with what
happens to you."

–Aldous Huxley

"Try not to become a man of success,
but, rather, try to become a man of value."

–Albert Einstein

"Strategy is a fancy word for coming up with a long-term plan and putting it into action."

–Ellie Pidot

"Strategy without process is little more than a wish list."

–Robert Filek

"Progress involves taking risks. You can't steal
second base and keep your foot on first."

–Frederick Wilcox

"Happiness is a byproduct of optimism."

–Tony Robbins

THOUGHTS

_____

_____

_____

_____

_____

_____

_____

_____

_____

_____

_____

_____

_____

_____

_____

_____

SINGLE SEAT GRATITUDE

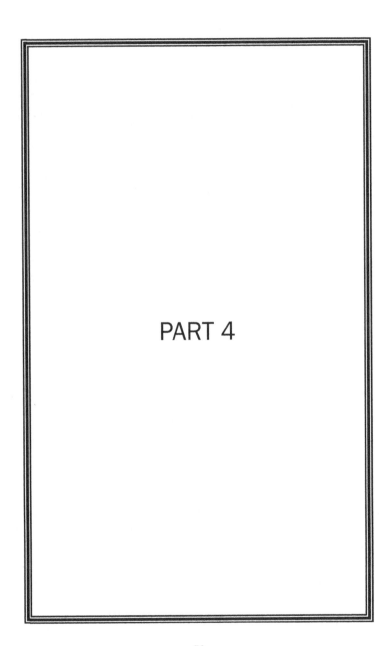

PART 4

HUMOROUS QUOTES

"Flying isn't dangerous.
Crashing is what's dangerous."

—Anonymous

"There cannot be a crisis next week.
My schedule is already full."

–Henry Kissinger

"If you're going to do something tonight that you'll be sorry for tomorrow morning, sleep late."

–Henny Youngman

"If I'd known I was going to live this long,
I would have taken better care of myself."

–Phil Harris

"For every action, there is an equal or opposite criticism."

–Anonymous

"I had a great idea this morning,
but I didn't like it."

–Sam Goldwyn

"If black boxes survive air crashes, why don't they make the whole plane out of that stuff?"

–George Carlin

"The only mystery in life is why the kamikaze pilots wore helmets."

–Al McGuire

"What is the similarity between air traffic controllers and pilots? If a pilot screws up, the pilot dies; if the air traffic controller screws up, the pilot dies."

–Anonymous

"The propeller is just a big fan in front of the plane used to keep the pilot cool. When it stops, you can actually watch the pilot start sweating."

–Anonymous

"Comedy is acting out optimism."

–Robin Williams

"Humor is laughing at what you haven't got
when you ought to have it."

–Langston Hughes

"Humor is perhaps a sense of intellectual perspective; an awareness that some things are really
important, others not; and that the two kinds are
most oddly jumbled in everyday affairs."

–Christopher Morley

"How does the moon cut his hair? Eclipse it."

–Anonymous

"How does the National Space Agency
organize a party?
They planet."

–Anonymous

Police:	Where do you live?
Me:	With my parents.
Police:	Where do your parents live?
Me:	With me.
Police:	Where is your house?
Me:	Next to my neighbor's house.
Police:	Where is your neighbor's house?
Me:	If I tell you, you won't believe me.
Police:	Tell me.
Me:	Next to my house.

–Anonymous

THOUGHTS

SINGLE SEAT GRATITUDE

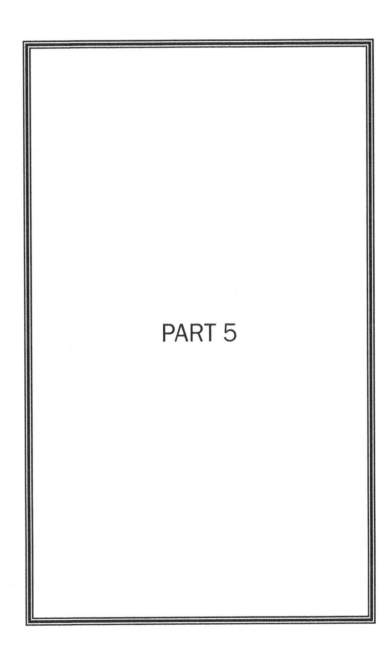

PART 5

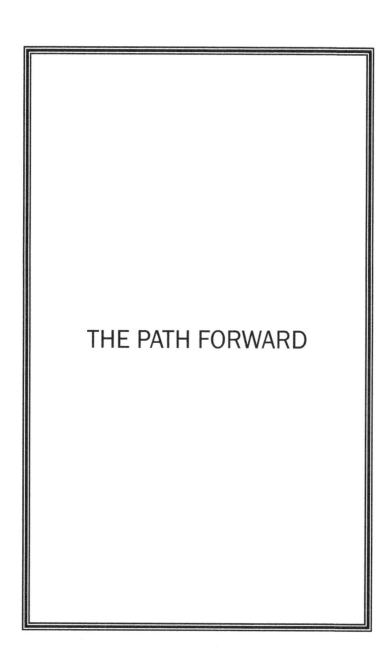

THE PATH FORWARD

HOW WE HELP PEAK
PERFORMERS BECOME EVEN
MORE SUCCESSFUL

What started as only an idea is now a reality. Isn't it funny how that works?

Listen, what I've been able to do is nothing special when you consider the facts. The facts are I've spent the last 20+ years of my life using trial and error methods to discover the secrets that I can GIVE you today for a small investment of time and energy. I'm not of above average intelligence, I wasn't blessed with above average skill, nor did I have any other advantages going in, other than the ability to work hard, re-frame my failures often, and never give up.

You can do the same thing I did. You can go out there and spend countless hours... dealing with all the stress, headaches and making all the same mistakes I did.

My question is why?

Why would you do that when you can shave hundreds if not thousands of hours of headache and heartache off by simply exchanging a small amount time for a proven flight plan to immediate success?

Breeze past pitfalls as we give you the cumulative equivalent of millions of hours of unique experiences, so that you can learn valuable shortcuts to achieve goals in a matter of hours or days, instead of months or years.

When you look at it like that, I think you'll agree with me that you're getting the deal of the century when you join our life changing community at:

SingleSeatMindset.com

THE NEXT STEP

Information alone is not enough...but you already knew that. I want you to think about your first day in school. It's the first class and you're bright eyed and bushy tailed and ready to learn. Your teacher walks in, drops a text book in your lap and says 'read this, I'll be back at the end of the semester to give you your finals'.

This happens with your next class, and every class that follows.

If that were the case, you would not be reading this today because you'd still be struggling to figure it all out.

Information is powerful, but on its own it's not enough.

You need more than just information.

- You need <u>tools</u>.

- You need <u>community</u>.

- You need <u>accountability</u>.

You need an <u>elite group</u> of fighter pilots to guide you if you're going to make it happen.

Once you make the first step by joining our impactful group at:

SingleSeatMindset.com

We'll immediately take you by the hand and we'll walk the first steps together, and then some...

How much stress does failing to reach your ambitious goals cause in your mind and body right now?

Poof. It's gone.

Can you feel the difference just thinking about it now? Well let's make it happen for real.

Join us today at:

SingleSeatMindset.com

ABOUT
DOMINIC "SLICE" TEICH

Dominic "Slice" Teich brings his civilian and fighter pilot background and applies them to help peak performers get cutting-edge results in a no-restrictions environment. Over the past 20+ years, he's created a number of products and services designed to help high achievers experience personal and professional success.

His flagship paint-by-numbers blueprint is called Single Seat Mindset™. This impactful community of fighter pilot guides joined forces to help those that are ambitions and sick of others getting in their way; they dive deep into the productivity world to help you reach your biggest goals all while avoiding overload, overwhelm, and burnout.

Dominic "Slice" Teich

You won't find any other cutting-edge product or service like ours as we provide a unique perspective for peak performers through our powerful group of fighter pilots.

Single Seat Mindset also publishes plenty of high impact content for high achievers, so make sure you request to be a part of our private and exclusive Facebook group and our Blog to learn from us as often as you want.

Discover more about Single Seat Mindset™ at:

SingleSeatMindset.com

P.S. If you need an afterburner approach to a difficult goal, our group is filled with peak performers - yep, you guessed it - a group of elite fighter pilot guides. There are multiple ways to use their unrestricted, no-nonsense, get-to-the-point approach.

Facebook:

facebook.com/groups/singleseatmindset

Blog:

blog.singleseatmindset.com

ABOUT SINGLE SEAT MINDSET

This impactful community of fighter pilot guides joined forces to help those that are ambitious and sick of others getting in their way as they blaze a trail towards success.

If you are a fast-paced, passionate, and highly competitive individual that wants to challenge the status-quo, experience personal growth, and achieve success, take the challenge and start to grow your mindset by using our no-restrictions, no-fluff, online community at:

SingleSeatMindset.com

To purchase another Single Seat Gratitude book to keep for yourself or give away as a gift, please visit:

SingleSeatMindset.com/books

A SMALL REQUEST

Thank you for being a part of our life changing community, Single Seat Mindset™. Part of our powerful strategy is to keep giving back...it's a great return on investment to help others and to see others you empowered helping people too!

This offer isn't for the hobbyist or the person who won't take the shot because they are fearful that they might miss.

This is for serious individuals who won't let anything get in the way of their drive to reach their goals. Yes, what I'm offering will take less than 1 minute, but in return that gives others a lot more—and isn't that what's most important? Giving back?

If this book has provided a useful service to you or anyone else, we'd like to show off your comments and inputs!

Reviews are the BEST way to help us and others push through pain, hardship, and confusion.

...so we all can BE better.

Please visit the following website to provide honest feedback so that you can help others achieve the biggest wins in the skies and on roads less traveled.

SingleSeatMindset.com/gratitude-review

If you have any questions or would like to tell me what you think about any of books or services, please shoot me a message here:

SingleSeatMindset.com/contact

WANT TO GIVE BACK?

If you are a fighter pilot and would like to become part of our impactful team, please contact us at the following link to become a guide for others that want to follow in your footsteps:

SingleSeatMindset.com/contact

All proceeds from this business are donated to charity.

To donate to the Anna Schindler Foundation directly and help families that have children diagnosed with cancer, please visit the following website:

AnnaSchindlerFoundation.org/donate

HIGH-IMPACT RESOURCES FOR PEAK PERFORMERS

Single Seat Mindset is designed specifically for peak performers that desire cutting-edge ideas from some of the world's most elite fighter pilots. I would like to extend a personal invitation for you to be a part of our independent minded community.

You can get all of that and more through our resources... most of which are no cost to you! Additionally, you can contact us directly to ask your questions that deserve a unique perspective unlike anything found anywhere else in the world...a fighter pilot's perspective.

If you are a peak performer with a *"Let's get it done, don't hold me back,"* attitude and want immediate results, please visit us at:

SingleSeatMindset.com

Put your talents to good use and accelerate past all the slow people holding you back from your ambitious goals.

Blog.SingleSeatMindset.com

If you are a fighter pilot and would like to become part of our team, please contact us here to become an elite guide and give back for all of your above average experiences:

SingleSeatMindset.com/contact

Made in the USA
Coppell, TX
08 January 2023

10706996R00069